HOUSE ON THE A34

Philip Hancock was born in Newchapel, Stoke-on-Trent, in 1966. He left school at sixteen to serve a City & Guilds craft apprenticeship. His debut pamphlet *Hearing Ourselves Think* (Smiths Knoll, 2009) was a *Guardian* Book of the Year. A second pamphlet, *Just Help Yourself* (Smiths Knoll), appeared in 2016. *Jelly Baby*, a film-poem, screened at various short film festivals and was published by *Areté. City Works Dept.* was published by CBe in 2018.

PHILIP HANCOCK

House on the A34

First published in 2023
by CB editions
146 Percy Road London W12 9QL
www.cbeditions.com

Printed in England by ImprintDigital, Devon

ISBN 978-1-909585-53-9

for Astrid

ACKNOWLEDGEMENTS

Acknowledgements are due to the editors of the following,
where versions of these poems first appeared: *Brixton Review of
Books*, *The Friday Poem*, *New Statesman*, *The North*, *Oxford Magazine*,
Oxford Review of Books, *Poetry Birmingham*, *The Poetry Review*,
Poetry London, *Prototype*, *Smiths Knoll*, *The Spectator*
and *Wild Court*.

Thanks to Arts Council England for a writer's award which
enabled the completion of this manuscript.

Thanks to the Society of Authors
for an Authors Foundation Grant.

Special thanks to Astrid Alben, David Allison
and Michael Laskey.

Cover design by Steven Aspinall.

The times have to be bizarrely lacking in interest for people
to get attached to my sort of literature.

– Francis Ponge

Contents

HOUSE ON THE A34

Man on the Fire Escape

Approaching the T-junction,
you can't miss him: white overalls,
one boot on a handrail
five stages up the fire escape jutting
from Tunstall library.

Next time you're passing,
his arm's locked round a stanchion,
leaning out, full stretch.
One slip
and he's through your windscreen.

Edging up one evening in traffic,
it's not the mullion windows
with pediment gable and arms,
nor the terracotta lettering,
just how far he's got.

Weeks after, the top coat
of lickable red blinds you
to that leaking-radiator brown
and you notice the way he breaks off
at the angle of strut and beam.

Today, stuck at the lights
between trucks, you can't help
but crane your neck, checking
the skeletal metalwork for him
even after all these years.

Old Bruce

Holding up traffic
by walking in the road,
still testing the tarmac
with his heel.

Even out where the buses don't run,
on crescents and side roads,
a limp you can't miss – wrenched
from the hip, head cricked to one side.

No one knows where he lives,
just the job he used to do.

Contract Colours

22

The woman who shoves the tea chest on wheels wants rose-red on her doors. She's sick of the muck that's been on them this last five years. We've not had a minute to check how the colour scheme will fall and she won't stop mithering us.

24

A big Alsatian lives here. It's had a go at everything including the lorry engine on the drive. Mr Ge'under keeps yawping at it to *Ge'under!* The doors will be delphinium like last time. We will paint them shut while the dog goes berserk at our steady hands framed in frosted glass. Blue on blue: no sweat.

26

Seawrack: a colour we don't know yet. Yucky brown-yellow. No one wants it. *I'm not bloody havin' tha'*, they tell us. We will decide – who doesn't behave will have it for the next five years. Despite his threats to report us to the council him here will be seawrack.

28

As the running order goes, this one will be gorse. A bastard to get it to cover and despite them down the office knowing this they keep it on the spec. It takes three coats to obliterate and it's still grinny. We swear they stick with it so we fail to make our bonuses.

Her doesn't look like a Tracey to me but we can't take our eyes off her. Curtains drawn all day. Blokes coming and going. Some mornings an HGV is parked up outside. Whatever she's up to is not our concern, only that we can't guarantee her the golden bronze she's fallen in love with.

32

They've seen lizard on the town hall and want lizard but lizard's not down on this scheme. They've looked after one another and this house since the war and leave us a drink and biscuits on the coalbunker. Once the Contracts Manager's been and gone, we might make an exception.

Blackpool

Red Swingball bats and the Disney-eye
of an inflatable dolphin pressed against
the hatch of the Renault 16 in front.

Lorries ahead, cabs to trailers to cabs;
faces at coach windows, all lanes blocked.
I slump in the back seat. We edge forwards.

I twiddle with the window winder.
Nearer the bridge. And see it: black smoke,
down the embankment a white car,

a man on the hard shoulder. Almost home,
round my mate's, tell him about the joke shop
on Central Pier, the Big Dipper, that car on fire.

Taking the Wheel

Halfords' de-icer in the glove compartment,
Easy Start, paper bag of mint imperials,
poking every switch along the dashboard
for the water squirter. Quick upright, arms folded
when he appears on the driveway: loosened collar,
cardigan unzipped. *But you promised, Dad.*
Nought to one hundred and ten: the dials
dead still. When his slippered feet ease off the brake
and clutch, I'm driving. I want Mum to see me
from the bay window, but he won't tell me again
to watch where I'm going. Careful of next door's fence,
steady, we dip to the grid outside the scullery.
Headlights: paint-spattered ladder chained up,
Baby Bio on the wonky shelving. I want to go again,
but it's getting dark. *Soon as you can reach
the pedals.* He drags the doors to, stops them
with the brick. But I'm already revving at the lights,
adjusting my mirror, pulling away.

Asbestos Garage

No more than six months older
than us, the deaf and dumb boy
who came by now and then

had scored a perfect pair of breasts
into the mossy back panel
next to our nicknames.

From the bus he went to school on
they all waved.
We gave them the Vs.

Lid

The job's to lever it open,
get straight on with what's in the tin.

But what clings to its underside
needs to be scraped off and added,

could make the difference.

Parks and Recreation

Dispatched with a spec
from central depot, we trundle the estates
in a clapped-out Minivan.

Re-entering astronauts, emerging
from its creaking back doors
in regulation whites, we take our gloss pots

to the slide, rocking horse, climbing frame
and teapot lid. Rag dry the tubes, bolts and collars
of the swings, unravel the chains

around the crossbar. Pick out the tripods
in lobster, mimosa, seacrest and delphinium;
work down the steps of the slide.

Finish the roundabout in apple. The horse
is tangerine. Mind our heads inside
the climbing frame, crawl out backwards.

Paint Shop

Craned onto the site from a truck
the ten-by-ten corrugated steel cube,
our paint shop. Nothing for sale
but a magnet for kids: bricked,
scorched, clambered upon, adorned
Stoke, Vale, obscenities from spray cans.
Inside the door, an Alsatian's head
in sagging red gloss welcomes you
to a throat-seizing reek of turps,
linseed and propane. Bowed shelving
to the left and right and straight ahead
an old door on two empty tea chests –
our prep bench – strewn with rock-hard rags,
clogged wire brushes, clotted stir sticks.
Underneath two five-gallon drums of gunk,
and the piss can. We referred to it
by its nameplate above the door:
Torton Strong Box, and down the months
more affectionately as the Torton –
our lightning-proof protector of paint
for gutters, soil pipes and railings.

Exhibition

An assortment of sticks
sprouts from a five-litre tin
on the work bench.
Plonked in anyhow
after stirring up paint,
they steep in a sediment
of turpentine and paint skins.

I pick one out: holly green –
the last colour it mixed –
clotted, knobbly, glistening,
an accidental Giacometti.

Pips and Stripes

Whisper the Deputy Chief Constable
was on the station, saw us heads down
on skirting boards, absolute attention.

The silence of corridors.
Any door that went: which shoes
were his? Nothing escaped his eye.

I tensed for any comment.
Chuffed to be asked to quote
for his lounge, to come round.

Pleased with myself, I got there early –
at a loss where to look, with him
got up in the full Stoke City strip.

Softwood

Two lengths of inch and a half
by a quarter, stacked one on top of the other,
planed: no splinters, no need to tape or tie them.
In one hand seems the natural way
to carry them – no bother.

Impossible to say how they come apart.
They break your grip, you hop
to use your thigh not to drop them –
hopeless, no way to bring them back
and suddenly you're the spectacle.

Guard Dogs

One of our lot slumped in the caravan,
while the rain kept raining, has done this.
He's shambled into the gloom and damp –
the paint-shop door grating on its bottom hinge –
and poked around for paint not skinned over.
With a clotted stir stick or a gloved finger,
he's daubed red ears, a V-snout,
splodged nose and eyes of what I imagine
might be an Alsatian and just legible,
Guard Dogs on Patrol.

His artwork on the back of the cold
corrugated-steel door won't dry for days.
Ninety-two blocks of houses to paint,
washing lines to creep beneath,
our swollen ladders killing our shoulders,
we turn away from the rest of our lives
to more of the same in the streets behind.
Yet, is it possible he's got home
laughing for once, not quite sure why,
no idea how to explain to his wife?

Wheelbarrow

Ten minutes would have been plenty
to scrape out the last of yesterday's mix
with the back of my trowel or a spade
and half a bucket of water to swill it.

Now I'm bent over the bed,
wielding a lump hammer instead,
then onto each side, as though bludgeoning
an unidentified beast, between my thighs.

Nylons

In the shed, I imagine
which workmate's girlfriend or wife
they might have belonged to,
the legs they once fitted.

I stretch one of the thighs
over an empty paint kettle,
tie it tight around the rim.

Pouring is patience: to strain
left-overs of the same colour
into one tin, free from rust, grit, anything
that would prevent a perfect finish.

Friday

After breakfast, our time sheets collected,
bonuses in the bag, the weekend begins.
Down by the battered garages
near the burnt-out Escort,
our apprentices go for it: first to find one
gets chips for his dinner.
Stanway says to take it behind
that steel-shuttered house, top of the estate,
and for all of us to be there, midday.
In the unkempt garden, we watch Stanway –
56, kids at uni, wife a pharmacist –
chucking bricks. *The wider the screen*,
he says, *the bigger the bang.*
One of the lads promises
an old black-and-white from his nana's
spare room, at last taking a real
interest, he can't wait for next week.

Above It All

A trickle in the street early on,
now spurting like a drinking fountain.
By noon water will be over the kerb.
Head gasket's gone on their compressor,
it'll be hours before they're drilling.

The JCB driver swings round in his seat.
They'll need a fuckin' lifeboat next.
Feet up, he flicks through the *Racing Post*.
Everything they're up against – clear
through his buckled cab door.

He only gets paid to dig.
Two hydraulic stabilisers elevate him
on this uneven ground, for a better view:
through-lounges, cleavages,
kids that want to be him.

Getting to the Top

No lift. Six floors
plus the Fire Exit steps
to the plant room on the roof.

You start off two stairs at a time.
By the fourth trip you're counting
the eleven per rise, the two rises

to every floor. Coming down
you remember which floor
by what framed prints on each landing.

It's all about your legs, the gaffer kept on,
what you need to think about is legs.
He'd told you a million times.

A long way down, longer back up.
So much stuff for such a small job,
you thought you'd thought of everything.

But now a weeping joint on the air con,
you'll have to get on to the yard.
Returning empty-handed –

not even a snack or a drink –
knackered before you've started.

Turntable

On the yard behind Hanley Fire Station,
Jean-Claude from the French manufacturer
is servicing the ladder. Bob, the chief mechanic,
hands slipped inside navy boiler suit
warm on his belly, purses his lips,
puffs his cheeks at Jean-Claude spinning
in the operator's seat like a funfair ride,
testing the turntable: sending the ladder
higher than the drill tower, maxed out;
then all sections sliding down,
gathered into one again, compact.

In the first-floor canteen
they face one another in silence –
Bob knows a spanner and a spindle
but can't do French, Jean-Claude
flummoxed by the local cuisine –
both relieved they're almost done,
back on their feet, *cheers, au revoir.*
Up there you're on your own.
You wouldn't believe the wobble,
even on a still day. You can spot fires
beyond the Potteries.

Brush Exchange

Locked in the boot of his Chevette
but belonging to the firm, enough brushes
to repaint the largest estate in Europe
twice. All sizes from the standard inch
to the seven-inch flat brush which was reserved
only for the few that could be trusted
on top work in town halls, the mayor's parlour.

One in, one out – a system devised by him.
We queued at his driver's side window,
noted the pinstripes worn from the thighs
of his suit, knew his smile was never a smile
whilst he decided which of our old brushes
still had life in them. After conceding
to those worn down to their stocks, or gone hard,

he'd bang on about the cost of decent brushes,
that he was doing us a favour, accused us
of using them on foreigners or at home,
studied our faces as though we were strangers.

A Personal Thing

In case any of his brushes
should go walking again,
he took care to cut three notches
at the end of their handles
with a tenon saw he brought from home.

The ensuing falling-out
when he wouldn't lend the saw.

e.g., Paint Scraper

Once done with his paint scraper
the most natural thing
would be to return it clean –

a couple of minutes rubbing
with sandpaper and the blade
would come up a treat.

Though given its clagged state
when he lent it to me,
how would he take it?

Calculation

Paired up for years
long before I came on the firm,
Bill always gave Chad a lift.
Wouldn't take a penny.

Your new double glazing looks well, Chad,
Stanway mentioned one lunchtime.
And next day – Chad couldn't work
it out – Bill just drove straight past.

Signature

Rather than who were picking up
the big bonuses, it was his signature
I'd look for when signing for my wages.
Just another bloke on the gang,
no particular accent or hairstyle,
but his handwriting – in fountain pen,
not the Sellotape-bound biro
dangling from the clipboard –
wouldn't have been out of place
in a shipping company's ledger
or even a book of hours.

Works Do

The Do Ron Ron: baggy-eyed and at 61 he's a bit long in the tooth to be sat around swilling Ind Coopes all afternoon. He's got some Santa Clausing duties later, so won't hang about.

Stanway: as popular as the plague but that won't stop him going. He'll plonk himself bang in the middle of the lot of them: if they're not speaking to him they're hardly speaking to each other.

JT: been on the firm for nineteen years and stuck outside wrestling ladders in all weathers for eighteen of them. Put him down to go: chance to sit indoors during works time, drinking.

Mr Bourne: not sure now because Stanway's going – they've not spoken since they had words over that one-inch paint brush thirty odd years ago. He won't go unless JT goes so he can hide behind him.

Robbo: is a definite, but first will have to set off his pigeons on the A34. He'll come in his overalls because he'll have to get back to see them in. Pigeons must be taken seriously: they always come home.

Big Ribs: after grabbing for everyone's bollocks, making them spill their ale down them, he'll sit up one corner and read *Boxing News*. Christ help anyone who cheeks him.

The Lad: if he looks too young, he'll be in the car park practising handbrake turns and wheel burning. Then the landlord just might see sense to serve him before a neighbour calls the police.

Norman: is sick to the back teeth of hearing about them golf clubs he didn't return to Stanway fifteen years ago. Any more and he will offer Stanway outside.

Zeb: might come but only after half four as socialising in works time is stealing from the firm. If he does he will have a juice; maybe the consumption of alcohol is frowned upon in Kingdom Hall.

Filthy Wilfy: will just have the one, maybe two. Being the chargehand, and out of the goodness of his heart, he says, it's only right he's there. But unwashed, in overalls: he's got a foreigner to gloss up in time for Christmas. He'll park his car streets away in case the area foreman drives past.

Lancaster: not his bag, but he'll turn up and sit outside in his Vauxhall Viva reading *Fiesta* until slinging-out time. Not for any game of soldiers will his son apply for a job on this place. He's got him down for uni.

Numphead: will just sit and sup and grin.

The Van

The back doors of the van
gaping open. I stop, astonished
at buckets inside buckets, upturned,
tiles bursting from their boxes,
crusted kegs of who knows what
and no ends to the electrical leads
snaking through heaps of dust sheets.
How could anyone know
what was in there or where to find it?

And where were they? Could be
they always leave it like this,
putting off opportunist thieves?
Enough time maybe if I'm quick,
out with my phone: steady,
click, a photo to check
once I'm well down the street,
relieved not to be caught in the act,
not to have to explain.

Delivery

After Clacker had roared into
the deserted school playground
in the works pickup,
he wouldn't budge from his cab.

He left it to us to flip the clips
to free the tailboards. We took our time
dragging the ten-foot sections
of Mills scaffold frames and boards

off the bed, while he sat
in a bubble of Radio Stoke, stony-faced,
his eyes restlessly checking
the dashboard clock, us in his mirror.

He burst from his cab without greetings,
as though ready to fight us, tugging
on his gloves, yanking each frame,
crashing them onto the concrete,

chuntering it wasn't his job
to be handling scaffold for painters.
His shiny boots going at it,
toe-punting, stamping fast the clips.

Door slammed, back in his cab,
reverses at high revs,
wheel-screeches away
to whatever site he was due next.

Arts & Sciences

A mop and a broom,
their stales cross-bracing
the corridor doors said no more
than I knew already –
how this caretaker regarded us:
No one's any business down there
as far as he was concerned
till the kids come back in September.

The art-room door shushes
into smells unchanged in decades.
Same green plastic spatulas for the glue,
the magnolia stop clock, long-arm stapler,
crusted bottles of poster paints,
packs of ribbed plasticine
and stack of coloured paper.
I will drop back, grab some for home.

Summer floods the science room;
the blazing bank of windows
south-facing: same nothing fields
where my daydreams vanished.
Crumbled lichen in a dry tank
of whatever was to be prodded
with pencils and noted. Test tubes
lined up like glass soldiers,

triangular flasks like Dr Jekyll's,
those fat rubber bungs and Bunsen-burner
hoses still look chewable. I covet everything
but don't touch: the art is to look.
Sleepless nights: being dug out
to explain a chemical equation.
Maths room next, my name and score
called out on Fridays.

Mesh fencing masks never used
on the top shelf of the gym store;
tennis gear we were not to be trusted with.
That suede-topped horse, tiny now.
Basketball: skulking so not
to get picked for Skins, shirtless,
puny against him in Adidas
the girls all fancied.

As though I had never left.
The caretaker will eye me
as if to say *I told you so*.
Those two wooden stales
were put there to save me.
Cut and run to get back
in case he's secured the doors
better this time – trapped me here.

The Caretaker's Mug

When it's not held by his big fingers
it can be found on the thin shelf
in his cubbyhole, beside the kettle.

Double the size of a regular mug,
stained darker than his preferred brew.
Never scoured, stronger than yours.

Snag Sheet

Cleat hooks glinted on the window wall.
We checked again the spotless parquet
for paint flecks, even the galvanised conduits
and trunking, the suspended lights.
A song of an American summer played low.

He slipped in ahead of schedule, mild, beige,
miles from his reputation. From a chrome tin
a telescopic aerial deftly linked
to a wing mirror. Straight-backed,
stepping sideways around the high room,

his eyes fixed on the mirror tilted just so,
keen to pick us up on any skimping –
beneath the cast-iron water pipes and radiators.
At his shoulder, the chargehand
feigned laughter at his own remarks.

We thought of the brushes we'd taped
to broom handles, to hooked wires
that got us to places we guessed he'd go,
smiled as we watched him getting smaller,
scuttling off without a word.

Special Effects

Particularly when shadowing
head teachers, market inspectors,
the clerk of the works: his talent
for laughing convincingly at any
remark they offered, or his own –
nothing was ever that funny. Too long
a chargehand to be considered
for foreman or manager, his attempts
to establish some kind of footing
or dress up reasons for his decisions
were often combined with comments
designed to humiliate the apprentice –
even this promising one they're surely
bound to promote to the office.

Breaktime

Mid-morning, shortcutting
through a back street off the main drag,
you're alerted by a high-pitched din,
screams piercing its ongoing.

No clear words,
more it's those raw feelings
learning to survive
inside the high brick walls.

You walk on, can't help
hoping for a whistle or a bell.

House on the A34

Suntrap bay windows
view fields and fields,
telegraph poles, a distant steeple.

Friday, just gone six,
you're heading north
on the dual carriageway

and there he is, stuck
on the opposite side,
car in the lay-by behind him,

holding his wind-whipped
jacket together,
a folder under his arm,

waiting for a gap
in the traffic – car after van
after truck – and already

you've passed, pressing on,
and he's left behind you
paused, still poised to cross.

Front Gate

Nose to nose, two iron scrolls
crown the top rail, dead centre.
Symmetry of box-framed bows,
barley-twist infills.

The universal latch
pierces the morning, the crash
a shock above the clack-
clacking of rush-hour heels.

Despite the stylish finish,
little attention has been paid
to the ways of water: where it sits,
rust spots impossible

to keep on top of. Never oiled,
the latch stiffens. And so it hangs
ajar all day, until coming home
maybe you take the time

to secure it behind you,
reassured that there's no need
to check over your shoulder
before fishing for your keys.

The Bench

It came with us from the other house –
in bits at the back of the garage.
Two lengths of scarred worktop
and its legs, which needed replacing.
A job Dad kept putting off.

Without warning it was down to me.
The battered legs I used as templates
for the new tenons, but thicker now,
knocked tight into the mortices
with his beechwood mallet.

Here and there the smudged colours
of my childhood – fence green, go-kart red –
set me off. I could have done with his help.
Why, once I heaved it upright,
was the structure rocky?

Of course, the uneven concrete floor.
Where it wobbled, slivers
of offcuts levelled it up.
Sometimes still jolts me
when I open the garage door.

Drawer

Nosing about in their room
for the Christmas presents, last stop
the bedside tables, his side first.

Everything you didn't believe. Like that
pink thing snagged on the reservoir outlet
Hassall poked with a stick.

Slam it shut. Scram.
Night after night you hold your breath
at the creak on the stairs, carpet

brushing beneath their bedroom door,
the light-pull toggle's
tap tap tap on the wall.

Bringing the Job Home

The tarnished brass knob off-centre.
Around it, the county cream worn
through to that 70s thistle colour.

Trace the hairline fracture
edging along the middle rail
from a screw over-tightened.

Notice that panel pin
waggled loose in the beading strip
from the door juddering in the jamb.

Next time, use the bathroom toilet.

Between

Absorbed by the TV in the corner,
the pair of us on the sofa –
but what of the space in-between?
The introduction of a rug or low table,
nothing to obscure the picture.
An emptiness remains:
colourless, formless in either light
or dark. Neither any use for it
nor to it, we stare ahead,
not seeing what's here or not here.

Slight Adjustment

Always on his side,
that's where it went,
the portable gas fire.

That permanent indent
where one castor ought to go,
the patch of pristine carpet.

He shouldn't have to tell her
the angle: not to scorch his legs.
But time now for his programme.

So he never heard the quiet
in the house, the slammed car door.
Couldn't believe she'd gone.

The Snow Thing

for Willem van Baalen

within reach of the back door,
leant against the wall
where you can get at it.

Worth closer inspection:
two brackets, four screws
clamping an offcut
of veneered plywood
to a standard brush stale.

It clears your driveway
in no time. Not a spade
or a shovel; let's call it
your snow-shifter – the least
we can do is name it.

Swilling the Yard

There's no better time
than after a downpour. No more
than a pinch uproots weeds
between the flagstones, moss
crusted on lower bricks
peels softly off.

No one except you bothers,
but starting from the far end
you swill pails of water,
sweep towards the drain,
slush of pearl-like bubbles
beneath the stiff broom.

You could sit and watch it dry,
but the gate latch rattles
and who the hell's this
traipsing across it and straight inside?

Spring

Clink of steel on concrete:
the tilted-back
cylinder mower.

Hinge

Split apart with a thumbnail
its two leaves open: brushed mild steel,
cool in your palm, symmetrical.

Allow a finger to settle
in any of the countersunk screw holes –
the natural comfort of cupping.

The definite edges of each leaf
will be bedded one day flush
in the door's back edge and the jamb.

This is where the work is done,
effortlessly transporting
the weight of the door.

Knuckle

When the leaves of a hinge
coupled by a pintle

are painted the colour of the door
so it doesn't stand out,

with use soon enough
it cracks, flakes off,

and keeps on catching the eye.

DIY

How much more straightforward
could it get, the exact fit:
flat-bladed screwdriver, slotted screw –

roller blind, curtain rail, door knob –
yet often it slips, gouges the wood
or plaster, stabs the steadying finger.

You're wild, you're flapping your hand,
it'll snag on your pocket, sting
slicing a lemon. You've done it again.

The Tool Chest

How much space was it really taking up
at the back of the garage? Flipped open,
on the lid's underside a handsaw
and a brass-backed tenon saw held fast
by swivel pegs; two shallow box drawers
with gimlets, awls, that yellow cylindrical tin
for the bricklaying plumb line, slid apart
to get at the bigger stuff, any old how
at the bottom: chisels, the brace and its bits,
that rod like a devil's tail – the soldering iron.

Hand tools for absolute precision.
Nothing electrical. Grandad's kit,
that had skipped my father, hardly needed
by me in the city, that top-floor flat,
so I drove them to the auction place.
No more lugging around, making space.
Never sell your tools, he always said.
The chest though could have gone on working
as the box I sat on watching him at his vice
filing each single tooth on the saw.

Autobiography

From first light:
the crack in the ceiling
above my bed.

Hard to gauge any advance
on yesterday, or last year.
How it falters, breaks off

at that sharp angle.
The comfort
of the familiar path.

Even where someone's
made good with filler
it opens again.

Offcut

Severed from the rest of what it was
I nab it, pulley-wheel it forty foot
to the top of the scaffolding. Just after eight,
the cars crawling over the flyover,
the sun will soon be level with me; here,
away from all forgettable activity below,
sat on this dry board I settle to my work.

What better place to be? What better options
for a board: a handy size for keeping out
next door's cat, mixing cement on,
boxing in pipes or as a speaker shelf.
Once I'm done I'll make it a Wet Paint sign,
or slip it behind the electric cupboard
in the basement for next time.

Smudge

he called it, money can't buy it:
concoction of dirty turps,
linseed, paint skins
and bits of bits from the bottoms of tins,
waste of all things alkyd.

Gratton checked its levels of settlement
in the squat ten-gallon drum
beneath our prep bench, reminded to
by the hum of its festering
at the crashing open paint-shop door.

How spirits rise to the top,
how turps turns yellow, and the sump's
a junk too greasy to set hard:
nothing reversible, every drop reusable
to save the firm pence.

A nameless colour. The art of pouring
is a steady hand on the tilted drum,
no slopping. Mung dolloped out
into our paint kettles. No need
for stinginess. Dirty work:

coating the insides of guttering,
to seal dripping joints, bind
furring asbestos, lubricate
rust-flaking iron and permit
the natural flow of rainwater.

Set in

Thirty-five years in the trade
and you believed you could read the sky.
Now the job's almost done,
it's as though you've worried it on.

In the passenger seat for a change,
at odds with the roomy footwell,
you can't relax into your book.
The laptops and handbags long gone.

From guttering to downspouts
to drains, how noisy it is.
God's way – your mother used
to say – *of making you rest.*

We Knew Him as Cot

Remember those lanes he walked after work,
past the weed-wormed car park
at the rusting colliery to the two-street
village, to catch the bookies
or straight into the Oak.
His days governed by dim light:
in boiler houses or the single-bulb rooms
of boarded-up terraces – jobs no one
wanted never phased him.

The same fanged grin at a rumour
his horse had come in, tipping me
for putting his bets on; the whiff
of piss even turps couldn't disguise.
No family, nor home, some nights
sneaking back to the job to doss.
He was found on the edge of a field,
crushing those tiny blue flowers
I still don't know the name of.

Light Work

The poppy-red panel
with four screw holes
on the door is softening
to the lobster pink
around it now.

At eye level
so as not to be missed.
You wonder
who took the sign
and what it said.

Wires

From reception
they followed stringboards
upstairs to the photocopying room,
through accounts,
into the main offices.

Miles of white wires
overpowering skirting boards,
pinned around door frames,
taped to woodchipped walls
or burrowed beneath fitted carpets.

Superhighways
off the spools of the intercom
or computer and trigger-happy
telephone men gunning on another;
electricians bamboozled

by which were live. Few takers now
for cable-pin packets on racks
in hardware stores; the skirting tops
are ledges for dust. We step
about, talking to ourselves.

Subway

Ribbed concrete ramp descends
to the tunnel entrance
deadening town-centre sounds.

Footsteps come into their own.
Faceless figures approaching
stick to their side.

The light ahead expands
as I hurry on up, emerging,
always surprised

how little distance I've travelled.

Knocking Off

The shapes I made, jags of pain,
contorting to get at paint scuffs
on the back of an arm or elbow,
rid myself of any trace of the day.
I could be at it twenty minutes.

Out of my shrunken overalls,
into a peach shirt, suede blouson
and practised grin. Shoulders back,
done with my slouched gait, scrubbing
floors with wire wool and turps

or crouched before miles of park railings.
No more nobody-man. No fear
of girls I knew clocking me.
Prancing through town after knocking-off time
as if I was on Boulevard de la Croisette

or had just stepped off a yacht in Cannes.
And though my head throbbed with paint fumes
that would take hours to lift,
my mind useless, I knew how it felt
to be given the eye, to be called *Sir*.

Dummy Drawer

Hip height, at the kitchen sink,
same alloy handle, same chamfered edges:

you still keep on trying it.

Ⓑ *editions*

Founded in 2007, CB editions publishes chiefly short
fiction and poetry, including work in translation.
Books can be ordered from www.cbeditions.com.